Addicted to Addiction: Chaos and Control

Breanna Laws

Presentation by *BookLeaf Publishing*

Web: www.bookleafpub.com

E-mail: info@bookleafpub.com

ISBN: 9789395756167

First edition 2022

DEDICATION

This book is dedicated to all those still struggling with their battles against illness and addiction. You are welcome within these pages, and your struggles are acknowledged. May healing rain down upon each and every one of us.

ACKNOWLEDGEMENT

This compilation is dedicated to all the beautiful
souls that walked with me in my journey of
recovery. You each deserve the same levels of
healing that I have been blessed with and more.

To Austin, for seeing me in my darkest and
pushing me to heal.

To Billy, Shelley, Holly, Dr. Casey, Kristen, and
all other staff of The Refuge, A Healing Place of
Ocklawaha, Florida. I would not be alive
without you.

To my little sister, Kinley, and all other family
members who supported me.

To Gracie, J'Lynn, and Jade — the ones who
never left my side.

To Cat, my beautiful girlfriend. We have gotten
through so much and will continue to do so
together. Thank you for being my mourning
dove.

And finally, to all those that don't feel like they
can make it to the next day. I hear you, and I

have been there many times before. Make it to the next minute. I love you.

Recovery is worth living for.

PREFACE

In this poetry collective, I explore my personal experience from childhood and into recovery. After years of struggling with untreated depression, anxiety, sexual trauma, panic disorder, and addictive behaviors, I finally decided to fight for my life again. Mental health is a confusing thing for a young child to navigate, and I hope that the first volume of these poems, which primarily focuses upon themes of my childhood and adolescence, conveys the child's perspective on these issues which are even difficult for adults to navigate at times.

The contents of this collection contain triggering language regarding topics of sexual trauma, assault, suicidality, self-harm, and eating disorders. Do not engage if you feel as though this could be unhealthy for you. Take breaks if necessary. Understand that these are things that I still feel sometimes, too. I am walking with you on your journey, and I am nowhere near close to the end of mine. I am grateful that I am not near the end. I hope you are far away from your ending, as well. May we heal together.

Home

Brooks Drive.
Hickory Run.
Old Highway 60.
Sawyer Road.
Berrys Lane.

Move to the next,
Escape the advances,
Gather up the photos
— The only evidence we were ever there.

Who is "we"?
When will "we" stay grounded?
When will "we" be happy?
Why can we never seem to function as "we"?

Newborn children birthed
To those unfortunate souls
Fighting to believe that
They can do this.

"We" can do this.
Though one of the "we"
Has barely managed words,
She will do this.

They cannot do this part alone.
They were never much for patience.
But her skin is still soft.
Her laugh still full.
Her smile still genuine.

She has no concept of these
Silly adult words,
So slip them in.
Every conversation.
Every argument.
Every opportunity.

She can absorb them.
Take them away,
Kiss them better,
Hold them while you scream.

Don't worry, mommy.
Don't worry, daddy.
You don't have to cry;
I'll cry for you.

It's okay.
I don't understand these adult words.
Throw them at me;
I'll hold them.
I'll take care of you.

Give you a warm body
When you don't let anyone else in.

Show all the kids how smart I am
So you never have to feel embarrassed.

Have my savings account open
Every time yours runs out.

Take everything; find joy in me.
Let me save you.
I can save you.

I'm so proud of you…
"We" did it.

True Love

Say I love you
When you get out the car
Give a quick kiss
Going to the same bed

Yell across the room
When the other fucks up
Under-breath whispers
Annoyed at the quirks
You once found endearing

Coexist.
Sit beside one another
— Smiling in family photos
Framed up upon the walls
Of that ghastly embarrassment
You call a house.

Use your human punching bag.
Justify one-another's actions
When scarcely a moment ago
You dreaded their existence.

May I coexist with someone someday.
May I say I love you

Exiting the home, post-argument.
May I whisper under my breath
My qualms with their quirks
Only to kiss their lips
Resting upon the pillow
Adjacent to mine.

Imaginary

I hope one day
To run away to the circus.
Be the divine ringleader
In my own house of wonders.

Religiously practicing
My great escape
From the confines of
The kitchen floor tiles.

Harvesting joy from
The mere thought of
Being encased within
Another person's being.

Any but my own.
Let me fly away
On my self-made jetpack.
Allow me to transform
With that mermaid potion
I so diligently made
With the salt water and food coloring
From the high kitchen cabinet.

A traveling ballerina.

A teacher.
A mother.
Let me be anything
That does not require
Me being me.

Electrocardiogram

What is one to do
When their affliction
Cannot be calculated?
Has no diagnostic code?

Doctors tend to appreciate
The value of good news.
Little girls tend to cry
Not knowing the bad news yet.

Doctors become perplexed
— Not seeing the problem.

Little girls become desperate
— Knowing there is a problem.

EKGs ease the minds of others,
But not that of the afflicted.

Good news is not a resolution
More than it is a gateway
To an endless train of questions.

To the one paying the bill,
This so-called answer

Piques a sense of irritation.

To the one being paid for,
The worthlessness of the visit
Metamorphose into guilt

Heart attacks do not occur
In the chests of little girls.
X-rays and EKGs won't help.
They won't make you an exception.

Your heart is not failing.
The pain in your chest
Is not the pang of death
Regardless of if you wish for it.

Those shallow breaths
Are not another episode;
Your asthma has laid dormant
For many years now.

Heartburn pills won't work.
Pediatrician visits won't work.
Nausea pills won't help.
Chest x-rays won't diagnose.

Answers will not arrive
Until you grab them yourself.
And even then, little girl,

Not everyone will believe you.

I cannot heal you.
I can't make them stop
— Not even now.

But please understand that
You are not dying.
Little girl, you are fighting,
And we survive that fight.

Inquisitions

Funny how the times change
— How we advance every day.

Age twelve, holding the world
Within your own hand.
No restrictions; no apology.
The world works that way.

What a grown up girl
Absorbing up all the information.
I always liked dark mode
Because it reminded me
Of my childhood years.

And incognito is a fun word.
Rolls off of the tongue,
If you know what I mean.

To a curious young child,
The most thrilling adventures
Are those which are prohibited.
And who are you to deny
This youthful rite of passage?

They may not know the meaning,
But it is the words that matter
— The credibility of knowing
What you shouldn't know.

What more can a child do
Than giggle at the screen
Of a middle-aged man
Showcasing his naked body?

If it is funny,
Then it is not upsetting.
If they can laugh,
They may forget their confusion.

And it isn't all bad, really.
Dark screens sometimes shed
More light than any other source.

Girl's giddy heart flutters
Upon learning that a girl
Could truly marry another girl.

The child giggles again,
Though this time
Not in confusion
— But in clarity.

Inquisitive minds

Will always find answers.
Curious children
Will always find dark screens.

May God help them.
And may we thank God
For secret searches.

Guidance Counselors

I have always had
A knack for lying.
My charismatic nature,
My paper perfect identity
— No one would bat an eye.

So lying to you was easy.
One of the easiest lies
I have ever formulated.

It is easy to smile.
Easy to say thank you
For all your praises.

It is easy to tell you
That teachers overreact.
That I am "a perfectionist"
— Just dedicated to learning.

I have never panicked
At an interview
Because it is so simple
To remain marketable.
My brain is the best PR team.

I would make a good politician.
Sweeping shit under rugs
Is childsplay in my book.

I would like to offer thanks
To every guidance counselor
Who bought into my campaign.
It was a pleasure doing business.
I appreciate your flattery.

Your brilliant smiles
Upon pulling up my grades,
Your confused faces
At my alleged suicidality,
Are making me blush.

You are too kind.
— So good at your job.
It has been such an honor
To have fifteen minutes
Of your appraisal.

Thank you for your guidance.
Look forward to next time.

Best,

Breanna

Schooldays

Boredom can be salvation
When boredom seems to be
Your sole talent.

I can be bored.
I can look at a board.
I can board up my curiosity.
I can be praised by the board.

Who needs a God
When you have 1060 Lexile
In third grade?

What threat is Satan
When you can fail a test?
— Fail at your one talent?

A blessing to be bored —
To be held in a board,
But boards always have borders,
And the souls of the curious
Have never done well with borders.

Eventually, they all slip.
Their chalk capabilities

Brushed away by soft felt
That somehow feels like torture.

People ask me who I am.
What I do.
What I love.
What my assets are.
What I can do.

The truth is unclear.
I am brilliant,
A genius,
Talented,
And all the things
A soul could want.

But unless I have a board
To showcase my skills…
Unless I have a board
To validate my success…
Unless I am bored
Wasting away in the institution…

Then maybe I don't have anything at all.

Sam

Elementary innocence.
Middle school hormones.
An uncrowded park at sunset.
A long gravel trail.

Our parents can't see
The children out on the trail.
Our parents can't see
The way the male child
Spoke to me.

"Let me show you"
— Such romance.

Men are always forward.
Men always know.
Men hold the power.
Chivalry is not dead.

I know it is not dead
As his hands grab my hood
— Rejecting my refusal.

I simply could not see

The true romance at the time
As his face desperately tried
To unify with mine.

Perhaps I am immature.
I cannot see the love here.
I am just too shy
To receive the male advances.

Yes, that must be why.

I will grow into love.
One day form crushes.
Maybe even see my foolishness
In this private moment.

To reject advances
Is a sign of disrespect.
I never meant to do this
— To disrespect my friend.

I feel sorry for my actions,
But I will not see him again
— Never able to apologize.

Maybe that's why I cried.
Why I stayed so silent
On the drive home.
Why I felt so repulsive.

It must have been my fault
For not seeing this moment
The way it was intended.

He said he loved me.
He told me he wanted me.
Should I have accepted this?
Taken his chivalry at face value?

I guess this is the way
— This is how boys behave.

This is how boys talk.
How boys flirt.
How boys love.

How stupid I must be
To reject boy love.

How strange I must be
To recoil at boy flirts.

How unkind I must be
To turn away from boy talk.

How foolish I must be
To expect different
Of boy behavior.

So, goodnight, boy friend.
I am sorry I ruined this.
I know we won't talk again.

Don't worry, I promise.
I will remember boy love.
And I will accept this form
Of boy love someday.

This is how boys must love
— Right?

The Reality of Fantasy

Do your memories fade?
Do they hold on too strong?
Does your little world
Have as many gaps as mine?

Do you find yourself in places
No clue how you arrived?
Do you run off the road
Two miles up from where you left off?

Do you think about parties?
About drinking until you die?
About loving until you can't?
About gambling your life away?

Do you think about wealth?
Do you know what the kitchen
Of your future mansion
Will look like?

I hope mine has big windows,
And a breakfast nook,
And little flower vases,
And old wood cabinets.

...How did I get here again?

I am so thankful
He let me stay on my back.
I would have never noticed
How nice his dresser looked
From another angle.

I wonder how it was made?
I wonder if it's hand-carved?
I wonder if the drawers creak
When you open them?

I could spend many long minutes
Scrutinizing this dresser
— And I do.

I can perceive these throbs
To be the pain of the stomach.

It's too bad I can't see blood
As a substance other than what it is.

God and His Plan

The most powerful prayers
Come from bloodied-up knees,
A pounding chest,
And anguished cries.

Those which sit
In quiet contemplation
Simply are not trying enough.
Not releasing their prayers
In a way which is good enough.

But not me.
I pray harder
Than any of you fuckers.
I talk to God
Better than anyone.

I scream to God.
I cry to God.
I bleed for God.
I bet you don't bleed
For your precious creator.

Cowards.
Fucking cowards.

I'm not like you.
I'll kill myself for God.
I bet you wouldn't do that.

God doesn't say much,
But I am sure He is there.
He has to be.
He has to be.

You have to be.
God, where are you?
God, I scream for you.
I cry for you.
I bleed for you.

My knees are bloodied.
My chest is hollow.
My mind is overflowing.
My throat is dry.

I am doing such a good job.

Why am I not yet clean?
I can't scrub it away, God
— Not on my own.

If I must stay dirty,
Then please take me now.
Please lock me away

Somewhere I can't sin again.

Gouge out my eyes
Which lust for the alike.
Rework my sinful heart
Which loves incorrectly.

This can't be your plan.
This must be my plan.
Help me stop following my plan.
I want to follow yours.

…

…

…

…

God?

Thank you for not answering.
I found the answer on my own.
Thank you for my ability
To find my own answers.

Tangerine

So funny
How easily skin peels.
How easily skin bruises.
How easily skin bursts and breaks.
How easily skin can accept punishment
From other points of skin.

If I strip the skin in segments,
Perhaps I could finally rest
Knowing that my outside
Matches my inside
I was never a complete self, anyway.

Citrus dreams
Remove the layers
Scrub it raw so it grows back tough.
Strip it bare so no one may probe it.
Make it bleed
So you may choke on your own blood.
Drain it.

Pick at the surface — spend hours
Pick at the surface.
How dare you have bumps?
How dare you be soft?

How dare you consume space?
How dare you pump warm blood
Out of your depleted heart?

Break yourself down
To the very marrow of your bones.
To the singular cells
Inhabiting your wretched vessel.

What a disgrace.
Who are you to give yourself
The right to exist in comfort?

Bring yourself what you deserve.
Cry – Go ahead — cry.
So weak.
If you can't handle this
What can you handle?

Does the tangerine sob
As you strip it raw?
As you tear into its flesh?
Why are you crying?

Stop crying.

Stop being weak.

Stop mending your wounds.

Stop hiding them.

Let the world know
Of your sick little rituals.
Let yourself fester in infection.
Bleed yourself dry.
And be lowered into the grave
A mess of skin strips, scabs, and blood.

Passions

I wish I could feel love
Towards my successes
In a way that is not forced.
In a way that is real.

I want to love on impulse.
I want to smile as I learn.
To whistle as I work.
To sing as I succeed.

Praise is the only thing
Which keeps me breathing,
But even it can't fulfill
The sense of longing I have.

Maybe I can't do anything.
Maybe I was meant to fail.
Maybe God intended
For me to be the joke.

I wish I had gifts
— Something to give me
That illusive sense of worthiness.

Sometimes people tell me

I am gifted beyond compare.
But how can I believe them
When they have never had to fight
To be considered talented?

They have the hands of surgeons.
The hands of teachers.
The hands of famous sculptors.

They conduct research.
They speak words I don't know.
They build things I can't build.
They learn in ways I can't.

But me?
I can write.
I can have feelings.
And I can feel writing.
And I can write feelings.

I guess the Creator gave me
The hands of a writer,
But even with this knowledge,
I still don't feel worthy
Of bearing even that lowly title.

I watch as my colleagues
Go forth with their endeavors,
And I feel that pang again

That pang of longing...
Perhaps envy...
Perhaps just a pang, nothing special...

Nothing special.

Writing is not even man's
Primary modality of language.
— Linguistics 101.

So what the hell am I here for?

I wish to tell stories...
To influence the world...
Let the world influence my stories...
Let my stories influence the world...

I suppose that is my purpose
But, why?

Why, when there are so many
More worthwhile purposes
That I could easily grasp?

The people which pity me
Have these purposes
That I was not blessed with.

They teach the world
All new ways to prosper.

But me?

I shine a mirror
Back upon the world.
Not showing it what it can be,
But what it is now.

How fucking useless.

Do you remember the story
Of a fairy called Tinkerbell?
How she had such a talent
— Blinding glow around the hammer.

But changed her whole self
Because her gift was insignificant?

Well maybe I touched a pen
A naïve newborn
— And maybe it glowed.

Illuminated brightly the room...
Brilliant, iridescent refractions
Surrounding all sides of my being...

But if it cannot allow me

To bring the changing
Of the seasons...
Then I die I life of futility.

I have a gift and a purpose,
But the pang in my chest
Permanently ticking with time
Reminds me my gift is insignificant.
My life is insignificant.

Yet I write...
And I feel...
And I feel writing...
And I write feelings...
Because what else could I do?

Maybe, in my future,
I can figure this puzzle out
— Do what Tinkerbelle could not.

Maybe, if I pretend
Just one more day...
This fruitless gift
Will leave me be.

Follow the Leader

Trends always dissipate
Faster than you can reach them.
Faster than you may catch up.
Faster than any poor kid
Hoping for some sense
Of middle-grade belonging.

Trading in my sweatpants
For the new skinny jeans.
Begging my parents
For an article of clothing
I never even cared for.

Only to do it all again
When even these clothes
Weren't enough to keep me
On the good side of my generation.

And now the very clothing
That got me in this mess
Are the objects of their desire.

And the price tags
In little thrift stores
Only continue to go up.

But I have to keep buying
Or else I won't stay relevant.
Love is a commodity
That I have to afford.

I am not sure who is in charge
Of these new styles
Or these new price tags.

But I know that they're the leader.
And I know that they own me.
I know that my sense of self
Is locked away in their vault
— Only sometimes available for rent.

I can't afford to take out this loan.
But I can follow the bank teller.
Hoping that someday
I may finally catch up
To these quickly fading ideals.

Four Walls

The outside world
Hosts too much disease.
And I am much too young
To subject myself to fatality.

Many do not understand
The beauty of four walls.
Many do not appreciate
The sanitation process
They consistently undergo.

People say I am wrong.
That I'm too dramatic.
That I'm wasting my life.
That I'm too encased in misery
To see the beauty of the world.

But they are vastly incorrect.
My four walls are safe.
This is the only place on Earth
Where nothing may defeat you.

If I find myself wasting away,
Then I will celebrate.
— For at least then,
I never have to face defeat.

There is no one here
To challenge my victory.
A winner by default
Is still a winner, after all.

Why subject myself to violence
When I can be blissfully isolated?

I do not want to come out.
I do not want you inside.
I do not want to fight the world.

If I go mad in this space,
Then I will sparkle with delight.
Perhaps I can make a trophy
To celebrate this achievement
— I'll be dripping in gold.

You cannot see
That I want this to happen.
I want to waste my life.
I want it to pass me by.

And whether I wind up
In a different vessel
Or in the afterlife,
It must be better
Than the world out there.

Sunday Dresses

The exiles who had come
From the captivity,
Offered burnt offerings
To the God of Israel.

Ezra 8:35

Sheep numbering 77, pure
— Each without blemish
— Each to atone for man's sin.

Perhaps the death
Is worth the death,
If wanted by the omnipotent.

Perhaps the lambs
Felt a sense of peace
As their skin melted off
From their unblemished bones.

Unblemished, only to be slaughtered
Into meaningless flesh.
But what is unblemished, anyway?

Surely not these people.

They don't care about God.
Two hours spent picking out
Which Sunday dress will captivate
The eyes of the boys
In their Sunday school class.

But then again, I suppose,
Perhaps they are more like God
Then I could ever be.

God only takes pure sacrifices.
How superficial is it
To believe that pure fur
Can mean a pureness of the soul?

How amusing it is
That the Lord and shepherd
Has favored sheep.

How incredible it is
That his sheep
Have favored flock members.
— Like father, like child.

It's okay, though.
His sheep will be with him
As he accepts their pure exterior
Through their sacrifice.

The Lord is their shepherd
— A guiding force of love
— Their one true salvation
Forever and ever, amen.

They were made to sing for Him.
The illusion of serenity
Can only be achieved
By working in his will.

So the sheep sing praise
To the very being
Who caused their death
In the first place.

Social Drinker

There is little in this world
I would consider a greater virtue
Than to be in control.

But, there is one other virtue
That may provide the same effect.

...

When all those around you
Aren't in control either.

...

Blurry lights in basements.
Firepits by the house.
Merry droves of laughter.
Sexual advances made
In the security of the night.

Surely there is no harm in this.

When one is so consistently
Hyper-fixated upon control,

It is a natural expectation
That they will find liberation
With whatever it takes.

For me, all it takes is this.
Three, four, five, six.
Just a few measly numbers
I don't have to remember anyway.

And I should be grateful.
I have just as much control here
As I do anywhere else.
I handle myself well.
— I handle my liquor better.

Selecting the "Rarely" option
On psychiatric screenings.
— I'm just a social drinker, after all.

A social drinker that just parties.
And keeps alcohol in her fridge.
And drinks it alone sometimes.
And cries when she craves it.
And wants it at her worst.

But this is social drinking, right?
Throughout the course of my life,
Societal systems have harmed me
— Worked against me in every way.

So when this funny liquid
Begins to work against me,
I can still call myself a social drinker,
Because it is society
Which made me this way.

So, if they ask...
I can control my desire.
I can control it so well
That I get rid of it
In an instantaneous manner.

All I have to do is pull out the bottle.

Disordered with Dignity

Little girls are in their element
When encased in Barbie fantasies.
Doll-faced and iron-hearted,
My scars must be tied
With pastel tulle ribbons.

I can apply pink paper wrapping.
— Crease the corners tight.
— Smooth out the bow.

A perfect exterior on a perfect girl...

Interiors are no matter
To the naked eye of man.
— Many eyes are still yet naked.

Injuries are better covered.
Blood is better withheld
— Masked under gauze.

Bodies are more beautiful
When barely held together
Beneath a thousand bandages.

For little girls, though,

Bandages are not merely practical.
Pink plasters coating the skin...
Glitter-adorned tourniquets...
— These are necessary

The lady will take care
To sparkle in her trauma.
Blood spills out in cascades
— Not ghastly gushes.

Pink dye charges extra.
Glitter is an add-on.
No, not an optional item
— An add-on.

Do not be mistaken:
These things are mandatory.
But I prefer it that way.
We women love to glow.

I love brightening up the room.
— Showcasing my ailments.
— Relishing my youthful exterior.
— Happily hyperventilating.

Yes, at one particular time,
I had my dignity intact.
A true lady in the making
— Luminescence in my agony.

A tragedy it truly was
The day that I cracked.
My steady deterioration
Forming fissures along my skin.

It is hard to conceal
The death of my very cells
Beneath my pink plasters.
— Breakages caulked with sparkles.

While I tear at the seams
And shatter into glass,
I can only pray to God
That my pink plasters will hold
And prevent my shards
From impaling those around me.

Body

Too much a woman.
Not woman enough.

Femininity is a virtue
I feel as though I lack.
Femininity is a curse
Pressing down upon me.

Craving captivating curves.
Praying for angularity.
Hoping beyond hope
That the Creator's clay
Has not yet hardened.

Body, who made you?
Who messed up this badly?
Why would a loving God
Put such little care
Into its children?

Cursed from the start
To carry womanly flesh
In all of the places
This gift perceives as ugly.

Cursed from the start
To carry jutted bones
In a way that people feel
An explicit repulsion.

Body, who made you?
Why did they gift me
With a defective model?

Why does a loving God
Choose who may accept
The gift of beauty?

Why didn't they choose me?

Lies

Mom, I'm not hungry.
Mom, I don't want to swim.
Mom, I feel fine.
Mom, I don't like girls.

Dad, I just don't like socializing.
Dad, I'm not trying to upset you.
Dad, I don't care.

Self, you are in control.

Self, be perfect.
Self, you can beat your hunger.

Self, be perfect.
Self, the hurt will make you feel better.

Self, be perfect.

--

self, be perfect.
Self, be perfect.
SELF, be perfect.
SELF, BE PERFECT.

You lying bitch.
You manipulative bitch.
You fat bitch.
You stupid bitch.

No, mom…I don't want to talk.

Fear

Escaping from this moment
Seeing life in blurry details,
Solely focusing on the threats
Wringing out your chest.

Fight against it.
Feel your body bubble up
Filled with impulses
That are not even yours.

Fly away from it.
Drained of blood,
Yet a thick, heavy pounding
Still persists in your chest
And spreads to every extremity.

Close your eyes.
Freeze.
What you cannot see
Cannot see you.
A paralysis of the bones
Leaking through your whole being.

Dull vibration which occasionally
Fuels our body into movement,

But may also shut down our system
— Consumed by the static.

Our plane of existence
Is exposure therapy.
We have no other choice
But to participate.

To feel our stomachs drop.
To have our bodies
Overstuffed with beads
To the point in which
They begin to pierce our very flesh.

Fight, Flight, or Freeze?
Pick your poison.
Pick your prize.
For we never know
Which one it will be.
Success is always happenstance.

And all those "what if's"
Boils within our bone marrow.
The sickly inward state
Playing Russian roulette
As to how it may protrude outwards.